My third installation book, is like going back into a trilogy set. My first book was Singapore Boleh – Conviction, which I hope, will help to make a better world, without CHAOS policies. To reinforce a robust government system, with tough questions, to prevent weak policy been implemented.

The second book, Singapore Taxi Driver is about my story and experienced, how Law and Fairness apply to a normal guy on the street. Artificial Intelligence (AI) is the Equation, to make social justice and fairness part of government policies today, into reality. Everything in LIFE take time to mature, when the time come, it will be your turn, to sit on the last music chair.

This third book is the mammoth one, dealing with one stubborn government agency that refused to acknowledge their mistakes, time and time again, rejecting all common sense, logic and wisdom argument put right in front of them. A marathon race which started in year 2000, I am still running with Forrest Gump soundtrack, the music keeps me going. I hope you enjoy the music too.

That agency is call HDB (Housing and Development Board), which was formed in 1 February in 1960, that can of worms inside, is what I going to open to let everyone see, their PROCEDURE and REGULATION are all upside down. By putting the train engine BEHIND the carriages. Nobody is perfect in this world, we need each other, to correct each other weakness and encourage each other strength, to move up the humanity stairway and not to keep falling downstairs, doing nothing. I hope kids all over the world, in villages, towns and cities will learn to speak up when they feel something is wrong about their country policy. Be a light house to shine and sound the warning early, this Earth is your too.

NEVER GIVE UP OR GET DISCOURAGE. I like to leave this quote with you – 'If you can have friends to help you, good, if not, just depend on yourself. Don't give up. You do what you think is right. You stand by it, you will win.' S. Rajarathnam. Old PAP Guards. I believe in him.

BEFORE I forget, I take this great opportunity to thank Amazon Kindle Publishing and to All my reader, for giving me this chance to express myself in a book. A B g Thank You. Have a nice day and peace of mind always.

To the Past, Present and the Future, the captain of the ships, is always the last to leave. I always like story with a happy ending, for I am.

The Cook, Nut Thinker, Dreamer and Storyteller.

May my dream come true. I am not the first or the last ship captains. Destiny.

We are all here for you, take care. It is a privilege to serve you all

Once in a life time. Twinkle little star. HAHAHA.

The first 3 months of Basic Military Training (BMT), my platoon officer keep emphasized this word – Don't Give Up. BMT give you the opportunity to mix with different type of personality background. My platoon mates some of them came from gangster background. I remembered they open my cabinet, without permission and helped themselves to the cake that my mom brake for me, when after the first month of BMT. They took away some of my SAF issued items as well.

If you want to stay alive, better to lose all this, then get into trouble with them, good thing they leave me in one piece, other suffered because they put up resistance. Those days, you can buy SAF items in Golden Mile Food Centre in Beach road, to replace lost items. HAHA. I was one of the physically weak guys, last in my platoon in running, so don't play hero in front of those gangster. The gangster is not all bad, when you get to know them better, they have too much big ego to lose face, that all. Just let then be natural leader. Years later after we carry on with our normal life in private sector, if you will to ask me today in the event of a war, I will still follow all those street-smart gangster platoon mates of mine. They will know how to survive better than you. They teach me one important lesson in a confrontation, you only have 2 choices – A. Fight don't talk or B. Talk don't fight. If you choose to fight and outnumber, always go for the bigger size guy, you knock him down, the rest will hesitate, if not be prepare to get stomp and beaten up badly. If you choose to talk, don't look directly into their eyes, that will boost their ego point, they will think you are scare of them, maybe they will let you go free.

Years later I end up in this situation, surrounded and outnumber 3 to 1. I choose to fight. They backed down, without any incident. I add one more thing which my gangster platoon mate never teaches me, you MUST be prepare to die if you choose to fight, it makes a lot of difference in the outcome, because you give all you have, the extra energy level. I am not crazy to fight but there is time, you need to make a stand. As a taxi driver, I handle a lot of abusive, rude and bully type all the time, you just tell them this – If you want people to respect you, you must learn to respect yourself first. If you, yourself don't respect yourself, how do you want me to respect you? Normally their pride will do the thinking for me and I just keep quiet for the rest of the journey, to give him chance to reflect his behavior. That only work for sober people. 20 over years as a taxi driver, never get involve in a fight, cross my finger. So why I choice to fight during my younger day? After I finished my BMT, I decided I need to be fit and learn how to protect myself. I picked up Taekwondo and during those months of training until green belt, my instructor encourages the trainees to join a tournament. 5 of us volunteers. I was the first to crawled out of the training session and only one guy managed to joined the tournament. That trainee had Chinese kung fu background, good and fast enough to handle the sparring with the blackbelt instructor. I ended up with bruised marks, the blackbelt instructors will definitely has the upper hand experience more than you, you are his sandbag. It was a realistic training fight session; it gives you a chance to test your knowledge and skill. So, when I was outnumbered 3 to 1, in that 1 incident, when you display confidence, your body language will show on your facial expression as well, which why the 3 guys, decided it not worth the fight. Bully depend on number, no confident in themselves.

The funny part after we finished our National Service, I met one of the former BMT gangster platoon mate in a street night market. I creeped behind him and gave him a neck chock, the next moment, I was surrounded by his gang! Good thing I did not punch him from behind, all I remembered was he turned, recognized me and said – Guys, that my old buddy, steady ok! HAHA.

As I said not all gangster are bad, they believe in comradeship After we got posted out of BMT, we went for map reading in the farmland area. They decided to help themselves to the rambutan fruits that belong to the farmer. I and another course mate were walking right in front of them, suddenly as they were about to ran past me, they shouted – Run, run! My gut instinct was to follow without question first. Gangster don't run, in a normal situation. We ran all the way tilled the main road, then I found out the farmers was chasing us with sticks. Now that comradeship, even though I was not part of his gang, he still treated me like a brother. Where to find?

The moral of SAF training, if you don't fight together, you never know who your real friend is. We know each other weakness and strength, you don't need to know what he is doing in actual combat situation, you already know what he will do and what he will not do. Respect need to be earned. Some SAF officers don't live up to the leadership quality, they are there, just to complete the 2 years of National Service. My BMT officers all deserve my respect. I lost my SAF identity card during field training, every trainee was dead tire, I dared not trouble them for help, so I told my officer to charge me for the offend. The group of officers organized volunteer tra nees in single file and managed to found my lost ID. I was touched, by the leadership quick respond. When I was posted to a signal platoon and attached for my first battalion exercise, that evening I bought 2 red bean buns. After midnight we reached the training ground, in the land rover truck, I took out the red bean buns and I passed one to my fellow signal mate. The artillery officer came over to my truck and said, - WOW, got red bean bun? I was thinking to myself, I only left one bun to myself, how to share. I carried on eating, the next was the officer cold icily remark – Never mind. He walked away.

The next morning, we reached another training ground, trouble start, the same artillery officer came over and order me to dismount the heavy signal set from the truck and carried up the hill. My signal mate and the truck driver cannot believe the officer were offended over a red bean bun. In Peace Time, you will know which officer calibers, you cannot trust to depend on. That is life.

Chapter One

Before I share with you about HDB story, here is my poem to reflect my long frustration over all the endless walk to see Member of Parliaments, over 2 simple documents which common sense, logic and wisdom, was deny and bar away because MPs cannot bind what they see but choose to believe the words of HDB officers contradiction explanation instead. Tired MPs, no fighting spirit and life.

My appeal case is in the light

Before numerous Member of Parliaments, to deliberate.

I observe each nightly Meet the MP sessions, hundred weary sweaty faces

Q in line for a few minutes, sympathetic hearing.

Not enough time, not enough word to raise the dead.

I sympathize with the MPs and volunteers' efforts.

Each case beforehand, written in few sentences.

Not enough time, not enough word to raise the dead, over and over again.

I deliberated.

I understand your word, No ground for appeal.

No lighting can be grounded, with just a few summary words from the MPs.

So, here I am

To hand over my case to you, Sir.

Perhaps I may ground my case, this time round

And rest each our other way.

Otherwise my Conviction stay, groundless.

June 27 2009

Let begin this mammoth story from a mole hole. In year 2000, I sold my HDB unit in Tampines. Before the Lessee (that me) can hand over the unit to the buyer, HDB will carry out the inspection on the unit. On 15 June 2000, Technical Officer (T.O) Leow Ai Hwa came to inspect my unit and inform me, that 2 items from the Contractor Invoice document was not stated in the Permit For Renovation form. She said as the Lessee, I am responsible for it. The HDB may compound a penalty up to $2000 for the 2 items, that is Bedroom No 2 built -in wall and install 2 shower trays. First shocked.

When I went back to Tampines HDB Branch, to show that my contractor has indeed wrote on the quotation, she told me, I still need the Contractor Invoice to show proof, that my License contractor did carry out the actual work. I managed to find the Invoice and rushed back to Tampines HDB Branch, however, the counter staff did me the favor by photocopy the Invoice and the rest of the approved statement. He told me; I need not wait to see her. That day she informed me, that HDB will suspend the contractor, but fine me $400, the second shocked. The next day, when I called her to confirm, whether she did receive the photocopy, she told me that the floor plan have been submitted to HDB office for approval, if not I may have to tear it down. Third shocked.

Sir, I find it totally unacceptable to me. The onus of responsibility lay solely on the Lessee.

1. HDB officer and License HDB Contractor are the person, who are MOST familiar with the HDB policy on Renovation.
2. I doubt any Lessee, when they sign the Permit For Renovation form, do they UNDERSTAND the WHOLE dictum technical reference make on the form.
3. I believe, when Lessee sign on the Permit For Renovation form, it is to let HDB board KNOW WHO is the Approve contractor, WHO IS DOING THE WORK. I doubt any Lessee will Question the contractor on the DETAILS of the submission, rather the Lessee limited Understanding, is what the actual delivery of work done at the end of renovation. When the Lessee see the actual work done, he will then be paid for the approved work. That was that simple.
4. What I think will be the wise PROCEDURE for HDB to adopt and License contractor to follow, is to Submit the Contractor Invoice with the Permit For Renovation, together. This way, HDB officer can VERIFY in the beginning and later, in inspection of the unit after work completion.
5. Any missing details can be cross check with reference to the Contractor Invoice, of what actual work been done and what the Lessee is really paying for.
6. NOTE: I have checked with HDB Bedok Branch, that Contractor Invoice NEED NOT be submit with floor plan for permit approval. HDB officer are NOT REQUIRE TO INSPECT THE UNIT, after the License Contractor has done the renovation. (June 21 2000)
7. No need for all the dictum of technical details to burden and hassle the Lessee, which I doubt they will actually UNDERSTAND. It is best to leave to the specialist – that is the HDB officer and the License Contractor to Affirm and Verify, then Approve the renovation work done. I hope you will appeal the $400 fine that HDB said is for administration.
8. NOTE: That on the Permit For Renovation form, HDB officer are require to INSPECT my unit after Completion of renovation, under the last part of the form – INSPECTED AND APPROVED WORKS COMPLETION. That was in 1987.
   I wrote this feedback and appeal to Minister Mah Bow Tan for Ministry of National Development in August 16 2000.

HOUSING & DEVELOPMENT BOARD
ESTATES & LANDS DIVISION
PERMIT FOR RENOVATION

Serial No: 525920

Our Ref: TA/w 8288-0170-1-01

Date: 9/10/87

To   Lessee: Mr/madm *Chan Chew Dar.*

Apartment

Street Name

Singapore

HDB Licence No: BC 2395

Renovation Work To Be Completed By: 15/1/88

The above Lessee is authorised to carry out the following additions and alterations subject to the terms and conditions stated overleaf:

APPROVED ALTERATIONS AND ADDITIONS

A   TO LAY THE FOLLOWING FLOOR FINISHES: (Maximum thickness including the tiles must not exceed 40 mm)

Type of Finishes	Location in the Flat
	Living Room
	Dining Room
	3 Bedrooms
	Storeroom
	Balcony
	Others

B   *ADDITIONAL IMPROVEMENTS/FITTINGS:

i)   Metal grills of approved design to all window openings/balcony

ii)   Additional wash-basin in the kitchen/bathroom

iii) Additional wall tiling in the kitchen/bathroom up to underside of the soffit

iv)   Repositioning of existing kitchen sink as shown on plan submitted.

v)   Shifting/widening of doorway between living room and kitchen as shown on plan submitted

vi)   Construction of arch-shaped doorway between living room and kitchen/ living room and bedroom entrance* as shown on plan submitted.

vii) Construction of 63 mm thick hollow block stands for kitchen sink

viii) Construction of 50 mm thick concrete base for kitchen cabinets (Size 450mm X 450mm)

ix)   Construction of concrete dapoh slab as shown on plan submitted (Maximum size 1.1 m² by 50 mm thick) (960mm X 450 mm)

*   ✓ denotes items approved and X denotes items not applicable.

C   OTHERS:

i) _____

ii) _____

iii) _____

I hereby agree to abide by all the terms and conditions stated overleaf.

SOL INDUSTRIAL SERVICES PTE LTD

Signature of Lessee

Signature of Contractor/Company Stamp

FOR OFFICIAL USE

Non-refundable charges of $ 185/2 _____ paid vide Receipt No _____ dated _____

Prepared by: _____ HHMI/HMI

Authorised by: _____ SHMI Aso Neo T. M.

Inspected and approved works completed.

Date: _____

EST/AO/715

HHMI/HMI

CONDITIONS

1 Permitted Time to Renovate

1.1 This permit is given on the condition that all authorised additions and alterations are to be carried out and completed within 3 months from the date of the issue of the keys to the Lessee. This permit expires at the end of the said 3-months period. No additions and alterations are allowed to be carried out for the next three years after this period.

2 Payments And Charges

2.1 The lessee is to engage his own HDB licensed renovation contractor for the permitted additions and alterations works and to bear all charges and costs thereof.

2.2 The lessee is to pay the necessary charges for his contractor to make use of the haulage service, including the use of the lift, provided by the Board.

2.3 All charges payable under this permit shall be paid at the time of the issue of the permit.

3 Haulage And Removal Of Materials And Debris

3.1 The Board may permit the haulage of construction materials without the use of the lift when the nature of the additions and alterations and/or the location of the flat demand. Under such circumstances, the lessee is to personally supervise the haulage.

3.2 The renovation debris are to be placed neatly in the common area in front of the lessee's flat for disposal by the Board's Debris Removal Contractor.

3.3 Under no circumstances shall the renovation debris be thrown by the lessee or his contractor down the bin chute or washed down into the wc squat pan or floor trap. If chokage occurs to any of these, it shall be cleared at the expense of the lessee.

3.4 Under no circumstances shall the waste water, terrazzo slime or any building debris be discharged onto the staircases and/or the passageway in contravention of the Environmental Public Health Act and its Regulations.

4 No Damage To Existing Building And Fixtures

4.1 The lessee shall install and maintain the additions and alterations in a good and workmanlike manner so as not to cause any damage or injury to the Board's properties or the common property or any other properties. Care must be exercised in hacking out the cement screed so that no damage is caused the floor and wall, fixtures or fittings such as the wc squat pan, etc.

4.2 For installation of an additional wash basin or repositioning of wash basin and sink within the premises, the waste pipes shall not be embedded or partially embedded into the floor slab. They shall be installed on the surface of the floor. Under no circumstances shall the existing floor be tampered with.

4.3 All defects must be reported to the Board before any alterations or additions are carried out in the flat. If any defects are reported during or after the installations of the additions or alterations to the flat, the defects will have to be made good by the lessee at his own expense.

4.4 The lessee shall not remove or in any way interfere with the fixtures or fittings such as tiles for a period of 3 years from the date of the sale as per Clause 7 of the Sales Agreement.

5 Approval And Supervision By Authorities

5.1 Prior approval must be sought from the PUB for any alterations or extensions of the water or gas service pipes and electrical installation.

5.2 The lessee shall at all times abide by any law, by-laws, rules and regulations governing such alterations and additions and any other related matters.

5.3 The Board reserves the right to control and give directions in the course of these works.

5.4 The lessee is to inform the Area Office immediately on completion of the renovation works.

6 Contravention Of Conditions

6.1 The lessee shall forthwith at his own expense make good any damage or injury caused by him or his contractor and employees to any person or property in contravention of these Conditions.

6.2 This permit shall be revoked on breach of any conditions stated herein.

7 Indemnity

7.1 The lessee shall keep the Board indemnified against all actions claims or demands that may be lawfully brought or made against the Board by any person by reason of anything done by the lessee in exercise or purported exercise of the permit hereby granted.

SOL INDUSTRIAL SERVICES PTE LTD

SOL INDUSTRIAL SERVICES

Business Reg. No 348157/006
No. 349, CHANGI ROAD, SINGAPORE 1441
TEL: 4400871, 4406115

YOUR REF:

OUR REF: DATE 13th Oct 87

Mr. Chan Cheow Lian

Dear Sir,

RE: QUOTATION FOR RENOVATION OF 4-ROOMS FLAT
    AT

1. Three rooms and hall to lay ceramic flooring.	=	$3,600.00
2. Master room entracne seal up and open new entrance.	=	$150.00
3. Bedroom No. 2 built-in wall partition.	=	$180.00
4. Demolishing of store room wall, lay wall tile and ceramic flooring.	=	$330.00
5. Cabinet base.	=	$200.00
6. Construct kitchen stove.	=	$220.00
7. Construct sink with support ceramic tile.	=	$400.00
8. Install 2 nos. aluminium sliding door.	=	$640.00
9. Install 2 nos. shower tray.	=	$900.00

Total : $6,620.00

(Singapore Dollars Six Thousand Six hundred and Twenty only)

We look forward to your consideration and early confirmation.

Thank you.

Yours faithfully,
SOL INDUSTRIAL SERVICES PTE LTD

....

I, the undersigned hereby
accept the quotation.

....
(Chan Cheow Lian)

These 2 documents, the Permit For Renovation has a front page for Lessee, License Contractor and HDB officer to fill in the details and sign. The back of the Permit For Renovation is the CONDITIONS for Lessee and License Contractor to abide by HDB regulation before the renovation start. The other document is my Contractor Invoice, which show all the 9 items listed, which the Lessee agreement with the License HDB contractor to carry out the renovation.

NOTE: I have BLANK off the front page of the Permit For Renovation column under A – Approved Alternation and Additions. B – Additional Improvements/ Fittings and C. – Others.

The purpose is to make you understand what a first-time buyer of HDB unit call the Lessee, that is me, have to go through, to apply for approval to allow your License HDB contractor to carry out renovation work.

Does any of my Reader, looking at this blank off document call Permit For Renovation, UNDERSTAND how to FILL ALL THE DETAILS, correctly? As a Lessee, accordingly to HDB, you are SOLELY responsible to ensure the Permit For Renovation, either by the Lessee or License Contractor is fill up correctly to what renovation that is STATED on the Contractor Invoice.

The back page of the Permit For Renovation, call the CONDITIONS, did not make any mention who is RESPONSIBLE TO FILL UP, the front column under A, B and C. It d d not mention the Lessee, License HDB Contractor and HDB duty officer.

The last part of the front page of Permit For Renovation form, is state FOR OFFICIAL USE – Inspected and approved work completed, was not SIGN by the HDB officer, after my License Contractor has completed the renovation in 1987.

As the Reader, if you do not know how to fill up the Permit For Renovation correctly, is mean you are in no position of responsibility to ensure the HDB License Contractor, fill up the Permit For Renovation correctly, am I correct to make this statement?

The ONLY person who can assist the HDB License contractor to fill up the Permit For Renovation correctly is STILL the HDB duty officer, am I right in my common sense?

If the CONDITIONS at the back page of the Permit For Renovation, did not mention CLEARLY, who is responsible for filling up the form, will I be correct to say that the Lessee, WILL NOT KNOW IT IS HIS/HER, RESPONSIBILITY TO FILL UP THE PERMIT FORM?

On the day of submission of the Permit For Renovation, my HDB License Contractor and the Lessee, that me, together went to HDB Tampines Branch office at Tampines St 81. What happen, if that day, my contractor did not fill up the Permit For Renovation form, F YOU ARE, the duty HDB officer, will you choose to ask the License HDB Contractor or Lessee, to fil up the form?

What HAPPEN, if both the HDB License Contractor and Lessee cannot understand, how to fill up the Permit For Renovation form, who do you think, is the next best person to fill the form? As a Reader, I will think the next best person to qualified, will be the duty HDB officer.

According to HDB officer, the renovation contractor gets the HD3 License based on the number of years in his working experience. IT IS POSSIBLE, that HDB License Contractor, do not understand how to fill up the Permit For Renovation? My Permit For Renovation form WAS FILLED UP by my contractor.

Chapter Two

If a HDB Contractor need a number of year of working experience in renovation, before HDB approve his license, as a first time buyer of a HDB unit, HDB immediate ASSUME the Lessee is more qualified and experience in under taking, to ensure the written Permit For Renovation, either by the contractor or Lessee, the details submitted is correctly fill up, accordingly to the Contractor Invoice.

It is FAIR for the HDB, to assume the Lessee hold solely accountable for ensuring the details in the Permit For Renovation, is submitted FULLY, for HDB to approve?

What happen if the Lessee is not English educated or illiterate, how does HDB INTEND to hold them solely accountable in the submission details for approval in the Permit For Renovation? As a Reader, I will say the Train has a good chance to derail off the track before it reaches the end of destination.

What really upset me more, when you asked Minister or MPs for help, when you show them the documents and the first remark from Mah Boh Tan – It is simple English, nothing technical about it, you should be able to understand. Tan Soo Khoon – You are a educated man. You should know what you signed for. Below are the second set of appeal to Mah Boh Tan on Nov 15 2002.: -

Among the 5000 HDB workforce, only those HDB officers who work directly with the renovation contractor, will know which are the items REQUIRED for renovation permit submission. I can verify that because I tested the officers in HDB Bukit Merah and Bedok branches. All I did was to show them the 2 documents, Permit For Renovation and Contractor Invoice and asked them to identify which are the items were required for permit. NONE of them know. The reason why HDB has insisted that the Lessee is to be responsible to verify the Permit For Renovation and not the HDB duty officer or HDB License contractor is based on the HDB written law or procedure, under the memorandum of lease: - special covenants with and undertakes to the Board (whose decision in this respect shall be final in each case), do any of the following things or acts. My last meeting with Sim Yeow Seng and Ang Kwang Liang of Tampines HDB branch have helped me to establish some more facts: - There are no Instruction Booklet for the Lessee in 1987 when the key was officially handed to them. This instruction booklet allows the Lessee to be aware of which items are required for Permit For Renovation. The Permit For Renovation form in 1987, did not STATE who is responsible for verifying the items submitted. The HDB duty officer and License contractor had denied that it is their responsibility to verify the items in the permit form. The term of reference used by HDB to refer to contractors who have applied to work in HDB renovation is 'HDB License Contractor', which is misleading.

HDB Licensed contractors are not required to ATTEND any course or sit for any examination in order for them to get their license. The license is issued based entirely on their Working experience and the Numbers of projects completed.

Sir, I disapprove of the term 'License Contractor', since the contractors are not accountable for their actions

Unlike doctor, engineer and pilot in their different professions, who attend course and sit for exams, to earn their rightful license to practice. I will urge HDB to CHANGE the word or term 'License Contractor' to 'Approve Contractor'.

In addition, the Permit For Renovation form, make it CLEAR that the Lessee is solely responsible for the items submitted, as the contractor is not qualify to give written or spoken consultation to the Lessee, since HDB does not HOLD them accountable in their profession duty to verify the items submitted to HDB duty officer.

Sir, in 1987 I accompanied my HDB license contractor to Tampines HDB Branch at Tampines St 81, to submit my Permit For Renovation.

By doing this ACT or ACTION, I did seek the WRITTEN approval from the HDB duty officer, accordingly to the Memorandum of Lease.

The problem or loophole is, NOBODY was made Responsible to verify on the Permit For Renovation form. This is due to the fact that HDB procedure do not STATE, who is responsible for verifying items submitted by A. HDB duty officer B. HDB License Contractor and C. Lessee.

Sir, put yourself in my Shoes and try to Picture it. You the Lessee are ACCOMPANIED by the HDB License contractor, so you have no reason to doubt his professionalism. As the License contractor submits the Permit of Renovation and the rest of documents, to the HDB duty officer that day, the duty officer does not Sound or Mention to you any problem with the processing of the documents.

The HDB duty officer hands over to you a duplicate copy of the Permit For Renovation form, after he has collected $185 from you, for the administration fee and sign on it.

By doing this ACT or ACTION, you presumed the HDB DUTY officer has done a PROPER record of the document and there is nothing to worry or doubt about, that is until you start to SELL your house, Then the Nightmare begins.

TWO professional people, whom you never doubted their abilities, the HDB duty officer and the HDB License Contractor have actually SOLD the Lessee out!

HDB and the HDB License Contractor did a CON – tractor JOB on the Lessee.

HDB Duty Officer Role: - After 13 years down the road, when I decided to sell my house, got to pay the $400 penalty or admin fee, ONLY then did I find out what the HDB officer's main responsibility is, upon checking the Permit of Renovation form submission.

HDB duty officer main function is just to APPROVE what the HDB License contractor has submitted. He approved the items accordingly to Permit of Renovation form. It is not the HDB duty officer responsibility or duty to VERIFY whether the HDB License contractor has submitted the CORRECT item for the Permit of Renovation form or not! HDB procedure does NOT state so.

Sir, under this circumstance, will any Lessee know that the Permit for Renovation submitted is NOT properly documented in the FIRST place?

This loophole or problem must be CEMENTED otherwise, it will keep popping out.

Submission of the Contractor Invoice will COVER up this loophole.

Duty HDB officer will be able to verify on the SPOT, whether the Permit of Renovation, is submitted correctly to the Contractor Invoice.

No FUTURE argument or debate between HDB or Lessee as the Contractor Invoice is properly submitted by the license or approve HDB contractor.

HDB duty officer does not have to WORRY, whether the Permit of Renovation form was done by a license or non-license contractor, as the contractor invoice can be VERIFIED.

During the tenancy of the home, any Lessee who wish to renovate their home from Time to Time, have to submit Fresh application documents to include Contractor Invoice.

In this way, it will ADDRESS THE MAIN CONCERN of the HDB, whether contractor or lessee have violated the Permit For Renovation, usefulness of checking any unauthorize work that has been done after submission of Permit of Renovation or written approval of HDB.

2020 HDB UPDATE: When I was working in RSAF as a aircraft technician, whoever the team assign to carry out the installation or assemble of equipment, will carry out a independent check after completion of work and sign on the document. Then follow by a second independent check by another technician who has not work on the system, this double independent check is to make sure you did not miss out any details or system failure. If pilot report any fault before or after flight operation, whoever has sign or counter sign is responsible to answer for the problem.

HDB duty officer and HDB License contractor sign for signing SAKE, their signature carry no weight in the eye of the Law. It is a USELESS document that nobody verifies what the Permit For Renovation, the details and items are correctly mention or state accordingly to the HDB License Contractor INVOICE.

Until today HDB still do not admit or acknowledge that their PROCEDURE or REGULATION is wrong in the first place. I wonder how many Lessee face the same problem like me? I had kept my Contractor Invoice all this year after renovation, think of those Lessee, who discard their contractor invoice. I paid a admin or penalty fee of $400 because I retain the contractor invoice as proof that I had USE a License contractor. Those Lessee without the contractor Invoice, will pay up to $2000 admin fee.

How much have HDB collect for all those ADMIN FEE since the foundation of HDB? How Much?

As one civil servant said to me, HDB will never admit their MISTAKE. If HDB admit their mistake, they will set the PRECEDENT. Think of how much money, HDB have to pay back to the Lessee. HAHAHA

I am a aircraft technician. I am trained to solve problem. As my gangster platoon mate said in a confrontation, you only have 2 choices, for this story, I choose to TALK to you. If HDB meet Incredible Hulk, he will say – Don't make me angry. You wouldn't like me when I'm angry.

Ministry of National Development
5 Maxwell Road #21/22-00 Tower Block MND Complex Singapore 069110
REPUBLIC OF SINGAPORE
Telephone No. 62221211 Facsimile : 62257254
e-mail : MND_HQ@mnd.gov.sg Website : http://www.mnd.gov.sg

A Home for Our People
A Global City of Distinction

Please quote this ref in your reply

ND 311/4-88 (15/02)

Tel	:	6325 8684
Fax	:	6325 7254

23 Dec 2002

Mr Chan Cheow Lian

Dear Mr Chan

SUBMISSION OF RENOVATION PERMIT FORM

    I refer to your letter addressed to the Minister for National Development dated 15 Nov 2002.

2   We have considered your suggestions carefully. As stated in the Terms and Conditions of the Lease, the Sales Notification and the Application Form for Renovation Permit, it is the responsibility of the flat lessee to ensure that the renovation works are approved by HDB before their renovation contractor proceeds with the renovation works.

3   The HDB Licensed Renovation Contractors' Scheme was introduced to regulate the activities of these contractors to ensure that they do not create any nuisance or damage HDB property while carrying out renovation works in HDB flats. As the contractors are bound by the terms and conditions governing the licensing scheme, it is appropriate that they be known as HDB Licensed Renovation Contractors.

4   On your suggestion that HDB verifies the renovation invoices before issuing the renovation permit, we wish to clarify that it is not for HDB to verify the invoices/quotations as the renovation contract is signed between the lessee and the renovation contractor and HDB is not privy to the contract.

CERT NO. 2002-2-0245
to ISO 9001:2000

Chapter Three

HDB replied to my letter said my Contractor Invoice is signed between the Lessee and the contractor and HDB is NOT A PRIVY TO THE CONTRACT. Well said.

HDB had make it clear that the HDB duty officer is to APPROVE on the Permit For Renovation, whatever items is stated on it. In another word, whatever items not stated on the Permit For Renovation, HDB will have NO knowledge. Am I right so far?

If one of the items in the Contractor Invoice is NOT stated in the Permit For Renovation, can cause STRUCTURAL DEMAGE to the building, there is no way, HDB will be aware of it? Am I correct to say that?

I got my HDB home in 1987 and stayed until year 2000. That is 13 long years, HDB have the Audacious action to state that: - HDB does conduct inspections of renovation works completed by the Lessees on a Random basis and/or upon the resale of the flat. The best arrangement is for HDB to inspect UPON resale of the flat so that the unauthorized renovation works will not be passed on to the buyer. No matter when the inspection is carried out, if there are any irregularities detected, HDB will assist the Lessees to rectify the irregularities by providing them an OPTION to consider whether to reinstate the irregularities or retain it subject to payment of Administrative FEE if the works are permissible!

In their own words, HDB admit they can CHOOSE as and WHEN to carry out the renovation inspection of the unit, even though the Permit For Renovation has CLEARLY state that HDB MUST carry out the inspection after contractor has completed renovation.

Really beat me all these years, when I keep thinking to myself, whether my common sense, logic and wisdom is working in my head or my head 2 screws has drop out completely.

One by One, all the Ministers and MPs, I appealed to, all of them can ACCEPT the EXPLANATIONS of the HDB, without Questions? How is that possible in modern Singapore?

How in the world does someone want to find whether their COMMON SENSE, LOGIC and WISDOM is still working in their head and not have his head 2 screws drop out?

I am the taxi driver. I keep showing all those passengers who are willing to spend time looking at these 2 documents: - Permit For Renovation and License Contractor Invoice. I asked all of them this 1 question, by looking at my contractor Invoice, all the 9 items, do you know how to fill up in the Permit For Renovation correctly? HAHAHA. ALL my passengers have one resounding answered - HOW TO? That was a real reassurance insurance best policy I buy for myself!

I only completed my secondary education without a credit in my GCE level examination, all my education come mainly from my working experiences, special thanks to RSAF for training me how to use my birdbrain to Think and Solve Problem and to my passengers who is willing to teach me lifelong lessons. When Minister and MPs said my command of English is poor, they throw all the spanner and screwdriver at me to discourage and set me off course, on purpose because IT IS NOT SIMPLE ENGLISH, THAT I CANNOT UNDERSTAND, it is because it is too COMPLICATED for Minister and MPs, to get INVOLVE, I have to be CERTAIN that my common sense, logic and wisdom is still working alright, is does not matter what Minister and MPs think of my poor English. I am enraged even more, when I THINK of those ILLITERATE Lessees, totally at the mercy of HDB LAW.

Once I am certain my common sense, logic and wisdom is right, I WILL CARRY ON THE FIGHT!

I am not going to let common sense, logic and wisdom be lock up and chain like a guilty person. Someone has to make a stand for them. Social justice and fairness have a place in this world. Which is why I decided I am going to clear all the world mess, to remove all the CHOAS policies that is taking bold control of government body in villages, town, cities and country.

Starting with my own country call Singapore. Call Save Spore Project.

Fairness can replace Law. Law cannot replace Fairness.

Unreasonable Law attract Unreasonable people.

Unreasonable Law make it easy for civil servant and government

to operate without any resistance and opposition.

In the words of Singapore Old Guard, Dr Toh Chin Chye

"The written word is law, that's how the courts operate,

that's how lawyers operate, that's how civil servants operate."

"Words that are spoken disappear with the wind.

Five years from today, the people would have forgotten what the

Minister has said or assured them."

The old PAP Guards really look after the welfare of Singapore cit zens

Which why my grandfather and father choose to follow them.

Now they are been replaced and retired. Sad.

Nobody is around to make a stand and fight for the common people.

Minister and MPs does their paid job. Everybody minds their own business.

They all sit in Parliament, doing their job, it is not a duty anymore

Nobody serves social justice and duty. Sad.

That is how nonchalant civil servants operate with unreasonable Law.

Not a duty to change anything, is a day to day job, without gui t or conscious.

The world needs urgent change. I sniff the air; the wind of change is here to stay.

By jolly and jelly, the Time is right and mature. Unstable rocks will roll down the hill.

Let make a stand for COMMON SENSE, LOGIC and WISDOM.

**HOUSING &
DEVELOPMENT
BOARD**

Our Ref : TM/8288-0172-1-01
(AKL/mar)
Date : 25 Sep 2000

DID : 7809500
FAX : 7850100

Mr Chan Cheow Lian

Dear Mr Chan

EX-BLK

We refer to our letter dated 28 Aug 2000 and 18 Sep 2000 respectively.

2   Mr Mah Bow Tan, MP for Tampines GRC has requested this office to re-look into your appeal concerning the administrative fee in respect of the unauthorised works carried out to the above-mentioned flat.

3   As explained in our earlier letters, under the terms and conditions of the Lease, HDB lessees are required to obtain prior written approval from HDB before carrying out renovation/alteration work to the flat. You have carried out the erection of wall in the bedroom and installation of 2 shower trays in the toilets, without prior written approval from HDB.

4   You have been given two options to regularise the matter. You could either remove these unauthorised renovations without paying an administrative fee or pay administrative fee to regularise the matter. Please note that the administrative fee is not a penalty fee. The administrative fee is levied for HDB engineer to check the alteration work and update the plan for the flat as well as other administrative works by this office.

5   HDB does carry out inspection to flats. However, this is not an issue of whether the inspection has been carried out by the former staff. The administrative fee payable remains the same whether the unauthorised works are detected now or detected earlier. That is, if HDB had detected the unauthorised renovation in your flat earlier, you would still have been required to remove the unauthorised works or pay the same administrative fee to regularise the matter.

6   If you need any further clarification, please feel free to contact my Principal Technical Officer, Mr Ang Kwang Liang at Tel (DID) No. 7809508 or at Tel (DID) No. 7809500 for a discussion.

Yours sincerely

MOHD LATIFF
HEAD, TAMPINES BRANCH OFFICE
HOUSING ADMINISTRATION DEPARTMENT

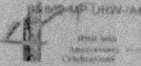

HOUSING & DEVELOPMENT BOARD

TAMPINES BRANCH OFFICE, BLK 510 TAMPINES CENTRAL 1, #01-250
SINGAPORE 520510 TELEPHONE: 7865555 FAX: 7850120

TAX INVOICE
GST REG NO. MB-6100007-1

SERIAL NO. TM 027189

COLLECTION ADVICE CUM OFFICIAL RECEIPT

PARTICULARS OF PAYER

NAME: CHAN CHEOW LIAN

ADDRESS:

ACCOUNT NO. 82880172101

Bill/Ref No/NRIC: CC code: TM

DESCRIPTION OF PAYMENT	AMOUNT PAYABLE	3% GST	TOTAL PAYABLE
PENALTIES/FINES (O)	*****$400.00	*******$0.00	*****$400.00

LEGEND: (E) Exempt Supply; (Z) Zero-Rated Supply; (O) Out-of-scope Supply.

DATE	ACCOUNT NO/ REG NO	RECEIPTING CODE	DESCRIPTION	AMOUNT RECEIVED	MACHINE RECEIPT NO
28JUL2000	82880172101	17270	PENALTIES	*****$400.00	TM186228072000

TOTAL *****$400.00

CHECK ALL MONIES BEFORE LEAVING THE COUNTER
THIS RECEIPT IS VALID ONLY IF IT BEARS OUR MACHINE PRINTED FIGURES

Find the work permit form, difficult to
understand and fill.

Name	Occupation
SUSLIZAH	HOUSEWIFE
Khuul Kaad	Shipping Officer
Lucy	HOUSEWIFE
Homidah Abdullah	Teacher
Flora	Housewife
Valerie De Souza	Acct Asst
Sheena Shen	FLORIST
Dan Lee	Executive
James Lim	Church Development Serv
Paul Tan	Sales Post manager
Terasome Lim	Student
CANKANI	ENTERTAINMENT MGMT.
NIICKLE	Nun
Linda	kd
Irwan sansuddin	Consultant
Nurdiany	Account
Ahmad Rizwan	Concierge
MD KIZ	Manager
Talentive Tan	Sale
Hod Rafie	Tea Analyst
Janet	
Mahendran M	(IT project Manager)
Bahar Begum	Clerical Officer
John	Creative director
	Student
Rojesh	Part-time Admin
Kilat	
Ucuuury	Estate manager
Tommy Leong	Student
Iggy Chan	Cook.

Find the work permit form, difficult to understand and fill.

Name	Occupation
Sandy Johannes	Consultant
Angel Chan	Product Manager
Jenny	Chemist
Thulasi	Clerk
Leudoa	Teacher
Ann	Manager
Michelle	Managing Director
Amy	Student
Ray	Cabin Crew
Constance	Customer Relation
Yap Pao Teay	Lawyer
Jeffrey Cheong	Engineer
Jaime Chua	Marketing Officer
Doreen Ng	
Jew Yu	Business Mgr
Gao Yang	Software Engineer
Joanne	Instructor
Cristina M.	
Ben Wee	2/1/02 Director
Serene	3/1/0
Jocelyn	Student
Jamie	
S Voegli	Sales Supervisor
	Manager
KY Lee	Sales
Helen	engineer
Crystal	salesperson
	Sun
Elsie Lim	Telephone
Ivy Ho	Customer Officer

Find the work permit form, difficult to
understand and fill.

Name	Occupation
KENNY J TAN	SALES CONSULT
JOHN SUTEDJA KASUM	
Chua Gek Soon	NW Manager et
Avon Gehan	
GABRIEL CHAN HOY SING	ENGINEER
Nie Wong	Self - Employ
Mary Tan	Sales Ass't
Peh Siew Ling	Teacher
Gene Wong	TECHNICAL MANAGER
Jason Siew	SYSTEM SOFTWARE E
Sharon	House Wife
Lydia	Buyer
Jason Tan	Sales Mana
MELATI	administrative
Colin NG ENG PING	Sales Creative
Julia Tan	advertising exec
avin Gan chee foe	Sales Rep
Lee Leng	Accountant
Paul Lim	Accountant
Maurice Yap	Manager
CHRISTINE ROSS	AIRLINE REP
Cassandra Ang	Marketing Exe
Noelle Ng	Admin Exec
May Chee	Teacher
BALBIR SINGH	AIR - CR
CHUA PENY	STUDENT
ROSLINDA	C/S
NORHISAM SOLAIMAN	ASSIT EN
Toh Soon Wa	System An
Oo Pek Gee	IT Se
Chris Lee	Banker

Find the work permit form, difficult to understand and fill.

	NAME	OCCUPATION
		Paramedic
88	Nur hidayah	
89	C. Kuhl	Software Project Mgr
90	C. Siccocie	
91	Fiona Low	Student
92	Richard Ng	SAF
93	JASON TAN	ENGINEER
94	Dr. Ci /CANG	SERVICES office
95	Kisha	BOUTIQUE MGR
96	Derek Chan	Comic book artist
97	H tan	Logistics Manager
98	Sharon	A/cs Exec.
99	Ria Diba	Secretarial Asst.
100	Dorothy	CEO
101	Jane Chia	Ast. Mgr.
102	Dennis	Sales Mgr.
103	LYNN LIM	
104	Edward Lee	
105	Sydney Fok	Admin Exec.
106	Richard Goh	Retail
107	Md Fahamy	SAF (NSF)
108	POH LYE HOCK	FOOT REFLEXOLOGY
109	Koh Khai Siang	Student
110	Affindi Hamzah	Consultant
111	Saharuddin Sausay	Civil Servant
112	Michelle Bong	Writer
113	Kelvin Chang	IT Engineer
114	Teck Shim	IT Engineer
115	NUR HISYAM	BANQUET
116	Rose	Housewife
117	vivien Tan	HR mgr

Find the work permit form, difficult to understand and fill.

No.	Name	Position
118	Grace Seavey	Secretary
119	Joyce Kok	marketing support.
120	Ishak Bin Hayat (MIDA)	Design Consultant
121	Jennifer Lee	Product Specialist
122	Belinda Leow	Lecturer
123	China Lee Kou	IT Engineer
124	Md. Mozf	Logistic exec.
125	Jan tto	Prod. Executive
126	Soorjana Rani	It Engineer
127	Cathy Teo	Financial Analyst
128	Blun	HOTEL / COOK
129	Jenny Loo	Asst. Logistics Officer.
130	LAURA NAPIER	TEACHER
131	Reginald Lim	Acck Officer
132	Cecilia Lee	clerical officer
133	Philip Tan	Loans officer
134	David	Teacher
135	Chandran Chen	Manager
136	Zurine Selleh	Admin Assistant
137	GINA KOO	CLERK
138	Alan Roberts	STORE KEEPER
139	Mary Ann Pieterusz	Bank officer
140	Chong Peng Siong.	Chemist.
141	Darren Lim	Web Designer
142		

Chapter Four

Google Dictionary: - Verify mean make SURE or demonstrate that (something) is true, accurate, or justified. Penalty mean a Punishment imposed for breaking a law, rule or contract. Fee mean a payment made to a professional person or to professional or public body in exchange for advice or service. Approve mean officially agree to or accept as satisfactory.

This is the letter which I wrote to MP Raymond Lim. 26 December 2001.

What the use and purpose of submitting the Renovation For Permit to HDB without the validity of the HDB License Contractor Invoice? HDB may as well, ask for a blank piece of paper or better still I can give them, my son's nursery book which make better sense.

Can you imagine, if I go to SIR (Singapore Immigration and Registration), submit my tenant agreement letter WITHOUT A. original work permit B. passport and C. employer's record, what will officer think of me? There is no way he can verify for me.

SIR office does not collect ADMINISTRATIVE FEE, free!

HDB collect $185 for Administration Fee BUT refuse to verify the Permit For Renovation with the HDB License contractor invoice, THEMSELVES!

Will someone tell me, what is wrong with HDB policy?

I stayed in Tampines for 13 years. For 13 years, HDB keep a USELESS duplicate copy of the Permit For Renovation, which is not VERIFY, a copy which cost me $185 – nonrefundable charges.

Chief Justice Yong has ruled that when employers or land lords make such a check, they must verify the documents personally and cannot ask others, such as employees or housing agents, to do it on their behalf.

That is the different. The immigrant act allows the employers or landlords a choice, to verify and certain themselves or go to SIR, to confirm if in Doubt.

HDB Act, ensure the HDB License Contractor and the Lessee to submit the Permit For Renovation, WITHOUT the Contractor Invoice!

If I were the judge, and when some irresponsible lawyers, who did not do their homework, submit invalid documents to this court, I will throw the lawyer out. I will make the lawyer pay his client, the original administrative fee of $185, plus cost of $400 which the lawyer fails to provide or substantial early.

CONTRADICTION ONE: - Misrepresentation of Word. Penalty mean Fee.

CONTRADICTION TWO: - Disregard of rule and regulation. Under the For Official Use, the column for Inspected and approved works completed, HDB has state that is a matter of choice for HDB officer to choose.

Can HDB say the SAME thing, if that inspection column were mean for the Lessee to inspect and sign the undertaking, were NOT SIGN at all, change your perspective overnight?

I hope all my Readers, understand what I have write so far.

As a taxi driver, I now like to say a BIG THANKS YOU to ALL MY PASSENGERS, who took the trouble and spend time to understand the 2 documents, the HDB Permit For Renovation and HDB License Contractor Invoice. They helped to give a sense of peace of mind, that my common sense, logic and wisdom is right on track, nothing to do with my poor command of English, in understanding in what s right and wrong in their HDB procedure and regulation. To all those countless civil servants from different government agencies, who dare not risk their career path, that I can understand, who choose not to write their NAMES and PROFESSION STATUS on the petition papers, I will still say a BIG THANKS YOU TOO!

MP Raymond Lim said it is a matter of TECHNICALITY. What he means is Law is a matter of INTERPRETATION. As a layman base on common sense, logic and wisdom, to me it simply means, IF YOU ARE RIGHT, MEAN YOU ARE RIGHT. IF YOU ARE WRONG, IT MEAN YOU ARE WRONG, NO TWO WAY.

LAW cannot fly, drive and blind common sense, logic and wisdom

Social justice and Fairness are here to stay, with so many people out there, who still believe in common sense, logic and wisdom. I wrote a poem on Law and Fairness, in my first book: - Singapore Boleh – Conviction.

Once again

I like to thanks all my passengers

for the morale support, to keep me running on the right sound track.

Thanks for all the encouragement words

to keep my spirit up high.

To think I hold belief in my Singapore Ministers and MPs

all those length and breadth years, in high regards.

All the appeal letters go to knock and crank

it matters nothing to you all, in the end.

My faith in my government is dash and trash.

Nothing stands in the way of unreasonable Law.

HDB Laws, I wonder who wrote them all?

**HOUSING &
DEVELOPMENT
BOARD**

Our Ref : TM/8288-0172-1-01
        (AKL/rs)
Date   : 15 Feb 2002

DID   : 7809500
FAX   : 7650100

Mr Chan Cheow Lian

Dear Mr Chan

EX-BLK

Please refer to your letter dated 9 Feb 2002.

2   We wish to inform you that under the Lease, lessees are required to seek HDB's prior approval before they proceed to renovate their flats. Under the renovation guidelines, flat lessees are also required to engage an HDB licensed renovation contractor to carry out the renovation works, including works, which do not require a renovation permit. The lessees are responsible for the renovation works in their flats. Hence, lessees are required to ensure that the works carried out by their contractors are in accordance with the approved works stated in the renovation permit.

3   We append our answers to your questions, as follows:-

Q 1, 2, 3, 5, & 6 : Answer - when applying for renovation permit, the lessee(s) and their contractors are required to sign on the application form. It does not matter who fills the form. The lessees and contractor who signed the application form confirmed that they apply for the items of works and agree to the terms and conditions stated in the application form.

Q4 : Answer - Upon receipt of the application form, HDB Branch Office will check and issue renovation permit based on the items of works applied by the lessees. Those items, which could not be permitted, will be rejected.

Q7 : Answer There is a need for flat lessees to submit the application for renovation permit as the proposed renovation works may affect the structural stability of the building and/or contravene the building regulation.

Q8 & 9 & 10 : Answer - HDB does conduct inspections of renovation works completed by lessees on a random basis and/or upon resale of the flat. The best arrangement is for HDB to inspect the flat upon resale of the flat so that the unauthorised renovation works will not be passed on to the buyer. No matter when the inspection is carried out, if there is any irregularities detected, HDB will assist the lessees to rectify the irregularities by providing them an option to consider whether to reinstate the irregularities or to retain it subject to payment of administrative fees if the works are permissible.

...2/-

- Public Service for the 21st Century   - Excellence in Public Service

TAMPINES BRANCH OFFICE
BLK 510 TAMPINES CENTRAL 1 #04-250 SINGAPORE 520510
TEL. 7800333 FAX: 7850100 Email address: hmsadmin@hdb.gov.sg

4   We trust that we have answered your enquiry. If ycu need further clarification, please feel free to contact my Principal Technical Officer Ang Kwang Liang at Tel 7809508.

Yours sincerely,

SIM YEOW SENG
Ag HEAD, TAMPINES BRANCH OFFICE
HOUSING ADMINISTRATION DEPARTMENT

RenovprocedEX862.doc(AKL12)

Hire the plumber, only if he's licensed

The recent water-contamination incidents at Bukit Timah Plaza and SIA Engineering highlighted the importance of good plumbers. **SHARMILPAL KAUR** *takes a look at what it takes for plumbers to be allowed to operate here.*

PLUMBERS here not only have to sit for examinations, but they must get work experience and face a panel of interviewers before they can get plumbing licences.

It normally takes one or two years for plumbers to get their licences, which they must have by law.

And members of the public are encouraged to check a plumber's licence before engaging them.

The licence, the size of a driving licence, should carry the plumber's photograph.

Officials explained the strict licensing regulations after it was revealed that an unlicensed plumber had connected a water dispenser to a wastewater source at SIA Engineering, causing 19 engineers and technicians to fall sick earlier this month.

There are two types of plumbing licences.

The Environment Ministry (ENV) issues sewerage licences while the Public Utilities Board (PUB) registers pipe and water-supply plumbers.

The ENV said that in order for registered plumbers to get their licences, they must first be formally trained.

One of the qualifications they can get is an Advanced Builder Certificate in Plumbing and Pipe Fitting awarded by the Building and Construction Authority (BCA).

Another is the National Trade Certificate Grade 2 in Plumbing and Pipe Fitting.

Once they have their certificates, they must undergo at least one year's practical experience with an accredited plumbing firm.

The final step is an oral exam conducted by the ENV's Sewerage Department.

The PUB's accreditation procedure is similar, but the requirements for on-the-job experience vary.

PUB senior engineer Kang Ngek Kong said: "With the BCA Basic Builder's Certificate, they have to work for two years before they can apply for the licence.

"With the advanced certificate, they can apply for it straightaway, though they will get their licence only after passing the interview."

The licence is renewable once every three years without further testing, Mr Kang said.

But licensed plumbers are sent regular updates on new legislation and industry practices.

"If there is a major change, we call them in for a day course," Mr Kang said.

Passing the oral interview is not as simple as it sounds.

Mr C.S. Tong, an executive member of the Singapore Sanitary and Plumbing Association, said: "Sometimes, our plumbers have to wait for five years before they get their licence."

The BCA said nearly 100 people received a basic certificate last year, almost double the number for 1997.

But Mr Tong said many plumbers tended to drift into more profitable trades after getting their licences, causing a drop in the number of plumbers here.

"Many of them can't get enough jobs. So they do other things. Only a few remain, so they charge more," he said.

There are 835 PUB-licensed plumbers, and 531 ENV-registered plumbers.

Plumbers not registered with ENV who carry out sanitary works can be fined up to $20,000.

Under the PUB regulations, unlicensed plumbers can either be fined up to $10,000, jailed up to three years, or both.

The public can contact the PUB on 731-3645 or 1800-284 6600 or visit the PUB website at http://www.pub.gov.sg to check if their plumber is licensed.

Sewerage plumbers can be verified at www.gov.sg/env/service/certs/sew.html

It is safer to rely on licensed plumbers, like this man repairing a leaking pipe in Redhill, than to turn to unlicensed plumbers.

COMPASSVALE PRIMARY

Two engineers get stiff fines for roof collapse

Seven foreign workers were injured when the roof of Compassvale Primary School's multi-purpose hall collapsed. Engineer Bill Hong (below left) and accredited checker Joseph Huang (below right) were fined.

Wreak untold havoc

'His failure to act properly can wreak untold havoc on the lives of many, sometimes long after he has completed his work.'

— District Judge Tan, saying that a qualified person in the construction of a building had a great deal of responsibility

By ELENA CHONG

TWO engineers were yesterday given the maximum fines for defective design and work lapses which had led to a roof collapse during the construction of the Compassvale Primary School in June last year.

Engineer Bill Hong Keng Chee, 49, was fined a total of $25,000 for flouting building control laws.

One of the three charges he faced was for defective design of the columns which caused the roof of the school's multi-purpose hall to fall.

The court also found that Hong had failed to keep a record of attendance book at the worksite.

He also failed to take all necessary steps in supervising and inspecting the building works to ensure that the thickness of the welding at the roof's steel joints was done according to the approved structural plan. These lapses took place between Feb 10, 1998 and June 15 last year.

The other engineer, Joseph Huang Wei Liang, 67, who is also an accredited checker, was fined $50,000 for not checking Hong's structural plans and design calculations for the building works.

He failed also an independent calculation to determine if the structure for the hall was adequate.

On June 15 last year, the entire inverted V-shaped steel roof structure of the uncompleted four-storey hall in Sengkang collapsed to the second storey. Seven foreign workers were hurt. One of them suffered permanent disability.

Yesterday, District Judge Tan Puay Boon also fined the building contractor, BKB Engineering Constructions, $30,000 for not ensuring that the thickness of the weld at the roof joints, which held up the roof, complied with the requirement in the approved structural plans.

In his judgment, he said he could not accept Hong's mitigation that he had delegated the project to a former employee, a qualified and experienced civil and structural engineer.

If the court were to accept this as a mitigating factor, it would tantamount to endorsing a working arrangement where a qualified person could delegate his work to another employee, without exercising reasonable supervision over the employee's work, the judge said.

"This would undermine the scheme which Parliament has put into place after the Hotel New World collapse, which was partly due to an engineer allowing an unqualified draftsman to undertake the design of that building," he said.

He said that unlike a car driver or other professionals, a qualified person involved in the construction of a building had a great deal of responsibility.

"And his failure to act properly can wreak untold havoc on the lives of many, sometimes long after he has completed his work," said the judge.

Accredited checkers, members of the construction industry and people responsible for putting up building structures must ensure that structures are safe, he said.

Chapter Five

I wrote this letter to Professor S. Jayakumar. Minister of Law. 25 Feb.2002.

Here are 10 INDIVIDUAL questions, which I send my feedback from HDB, for the minister, for query.

1. Is the HDB officer responsible for filling up the Permit For Renovation form. Yes or No?
2. Is the HDB License contractor responsible for filling up the Permit For Renovation form Yes or No?
3. Is the Lessee responsible for filling up the Permit For Renovation form. Yes or No.
4. Is the HDB duty officer responsible for verifying the Permit For Renovation. Yes or No?
5. Is the HDB License contractor responsible for verifying the Permit For Renovation form Yes or No?
6. Is the Lessee responsible for verifying the Permit For Renovation form. Yes or No?
7. What is the purpose of submitting the Permit For Renovation to the HDB Branch Office?
8. According to the Permit For Renovation form, HDB officer, are require to inspect after the contractor have completed the renovation. When do your officer carry out the inspection?
9. It is necessary for your officer, to carry out the inspection?
10. Is there a different between immediately carrying out the inspection and waiting until the day, the Lessee sell the house?

2020 NOTE UPDATE: -

Professor S. Jayakumar profile. He graduated top of his cohort at University of Singapore's law faculty in 1963 and joined the faculty as a lecturer in 1964. He was appointed dean and served from 1974 to 1980.

IF I were to hire Professor S. Jayakumar as my lawyer, and if HDB choose to answer each of my questions from 1 to 10, as a LUMP SUM ANSWERS, will my lawyer be ABLE TO ACCEPT that as an answer, to each individual question as the SAME ANSWER?

Will any of my Readers, be able to accept the way HDB CHOOSE to answer all my individual questions as one Lump Answer? Am I living in Stone Age?

I believe in Singapore Court. If I were to attend court, without a lawyer to assist me, do you THINK the judge will allow HDB officer, Mr. Sim Yeow Seng from Tampines HDB Branch, to LUMP ALL MY QUESTIONS as one individual answer? The judge will disagree with HDB officer and tell the officer to answer Yes or No, to each of my individual questions without I having to ask the judge for ASSISTING.

Google dictionary: - Append mean add(something) to the end of a written document. Question mean a sentence worded or expressed so as to elicit information.

My mom told me when I was young, she said, at home, you depend on family. When you are outside the house, you depend on friend and stranger to help you. That saying is still true.

My passenger who is a lawyer told me; it is not worth bringing HDB to court to fight my case. He said ust to get back the $400, I will have to pay a lawyer a few thousand dollars, even I win the case, the money I spend does not justify the cause. I told the lawyer, if I really go to court, it is not the $400, but my principal of life, never to admit I am wrong, when I am not wrong in the first place. The second main reason is to make SURE, HDB will eventually RETURN ALL THE ADMINSTRATITIVE FEE, back to all the Lessees. It is a day light ROBBERY WITH A LICENSE.

Sorry, my National Service, my SAF officers never teach me, how to SURRENDER, HAHA!

I have reached the end of my grandmother story.

I have done my best duty to my country and hope the future generation of Singapore Government, will have the CONVICTION, DUTY AND HONOUR to carry on the case for me.

After this year General Election, National Development Minister Lawrence Wong, as the main 4G spokesman said: -

"Our policies must always tilt in favor of the less fortunate and vulnerable. This is in the PAP's roots and DNA. We must never waver in our commitment to social justice, to preserve social mobility for all Singaporeans, and to build a more fair and just society. July 13 2020. The Straits Times.

I have a question to ask Minister Lawrence Wong and each individual MPs who won this 2020 election, do you and each of the PAP MPs BELIEVE IN WHAT YOU JUST SAY?

It is very important to me. What I see, is What I get.

If you want me to believe this government again, like my grandfather and father had in the past, you must have the moral courage to OPEN THE CAN OF WORMS INSIDE HDB's procedure and regulation again.

I can only open for my Readers to see inside of HDB upside down policy.

Allow me, to leave the last quote from DPM Heng Swee Keat: -

"This House must fulfil its duty, to articulate and debate policy options, to build better life for our people, and to advance Spore's place in the world. This is the mandate that has been entrusted to us by Singaporeans. I trust that all of us, whether in Government or the Opposition, will share the common sense of mission, to serve in the best interests of Singaporeans and Spore.

My colleagues and I in the government have listened to the voices of our people. We have heard and share our people's anxieties."

As a rookie author, my Mission is only the beginning, to make the world, a better place for EVERYBODY. Thanks, for reading my story to the end.

Below, is the original copy of the Permit For Renovation, filled by my contractor.

HOUSING & DEVELOPMENT BOARD
ESTATES & LANDS DIVISION

PERMIT FOR RENOVATION

Serial No: **525920**

Our Ref: *TA/W 8288-0173-1-01*

Date: *9/10/87*

HDB Licence No: *OC 2395*

To: Lessee: Mr/madm *Chan Cheow Liau*

Apartment Bl

Street Name

Singapore

Renovation Work To Be Completed By *15/1/88*

The above Lessee is authorised to carry out the following additions and alterations subject to the terms and conditions stated overleaf:

APPROVED ALTERATIONS AND ADDITIONS

A   TO LAY THE FOLLOWING FLOOR FINISHES: (Maximum thickness including the tiles must not exceed 40 mm)

Type of Finishes	Location in the Flat
Ceramic	Living Room
	Dining Room
Ceramic	3 Bedrooms
– d. o. –	Storeroom
	Balcony
	Others

B   *ADDITIONAL IMPROVEMENTS/FITTINGS:

i) metal grilles of approved design to all window openings/balcony — [X]

ii) Additional wash basin in the kitchen/bathroom — [X]

iii) Additional wall tiling in the kitchen/bathroom up to underside of the soffit — [X]

iv) Repositioning of existing kitchen sink as shown on plan submitted. — [✓]

v) Shifting/widening of doorway between living room and kitchen as shown on plan submitted — [✓]

vi) Construction of arch-shaped doorway between living room and kitchen/ living room and bedroom entrance* as shown on plan submitted. — [X]

vii) Construction of 63 mm thick hollow block stands for kitchen sink — [✓]

viii) Construction of 50 mm thick concrete base for kitchen cabinets (Size: *400mm × 450mm*) — [✓]

ix) Construction of concrete dapoh slab as shown on plan submitted (Maximum size 1.1 m² by 50 mm thick) (*900mm × 450 mm*) — [✓]

* ✓ denotes items approved and X denotes items not applicable.

C   OTHERS:

i) *To install alum. sliding door for d bedroom entrance.*

ii) *To seal up MBR entrance and re-open entrance as per plan.*

iii) *To demolish R.C. partition wall of storeroom @ kitchen.*

13/10/87

I hereby agree to abide by all the terms and conditions stated overleaf.

COI INDUSTRIAL SERVICES PTE LTD

_____
Signature of Lessee

_____
Signature of Contractor/Company Stamp

FOR OFFICIAL USE

Non-refundable charges of S$ *188/2*   paid vide Receipt No _____ dated ____

Prepared by: _____
HHMI/HMI

Authorised by: _____
SHMI
Ko New T. M.

Inspected and approved works completed.

Date: _____

_____
HHMI/HMI

EST/AO/715

Food for Thought

North and South Pole Ice Glacier are Melting.

1. If you look at your home refrigerator, the top compartment calls the freezer, create ice cube, by lowering the temperature to freeze the water in the ice cube box.
2. There is simple no way, to create that magnitude, in the open environment atmosphere to freeze the air around it.
3. WHAT IF, we install firstly solar panel, thousands of it on the North and South Pole glacier, to Act as a night or heat shield to prevent the sunlight from melting the ice glacier. At the Same time, use the solar panel to convert this Storage of natural electricity to act like a gigantic compressed condenser ice cube box to freeze the seabed water, surrounding the ice glacier.
4. This way, the Top part of the expose land of glacier, is been protected by the thousands of solar panels, acting as a sun block. Second the solar panels, provide the natural storage of electricity to Repair the Bottom part of the seabed of the ice glacier, the compressed condenser ice cube box will act like a multiple roll of fishing nets, to freeze the water around it.
5. When the seabed of water is frozen underneath the ice glacier and remain stable, you will Add more compressed condenser ice cube box to Expand the area, that way you protect and build the size of the glacier, faster and more efficient.
6. Hope someone out there in this planet, can Think of my crazy idea, see if can be workable to save Earth. Let the element of Nature replenish, the other nature damage. Mankind is to assist the Connectivity and be their hands and legs.
7. The next question, IF solar panels can store sunlight energy, it means it does help to Reduce the heating up of Earth atmosphere, that mean Global warming, can be reduce if all participating country, help to install solar panels in their country. Desert Land.
8. CO2 is the highest element of heat in the atmosphere. Google say once CO2 is added to the atmosphere, it hangs around, for a long time: between 300 to 1000 years. WOW.
9. NASA has developed a new technology that can convert the greenhouse gas carbon dioxide (CO2) into fuel by using solar powered, thin film devices. Metal oxide thin films are fabricated to produce a photoelectrochemical cell that is powered by solar energy. By converting CO2 to fuel before it is emitted to the atmosphere, this technology can mitigate the burning of fossil fuels.
10. That mean there is still hope for Earth. How many of this NASA equipment is needed to reduce the Earth carbon footprint? 2050, that not much time left, to convert CO2 foothold in the atmosphere that can stay from 300 to 1000 years.
11. We need to work faster and harder. Can government all over the world, COOPERATE?
12. Don't walk on water, when you still can walk on dry land.
13. My gut feeling, is that Nature is not going to wait till 2050, 10 more years, one country follow by the next country is going to face the FULL IMPACT OF NATURE FURY, the rest of the world will panic, by then worry and despair will not help, we can only watch with fear.